The U.S. Territories

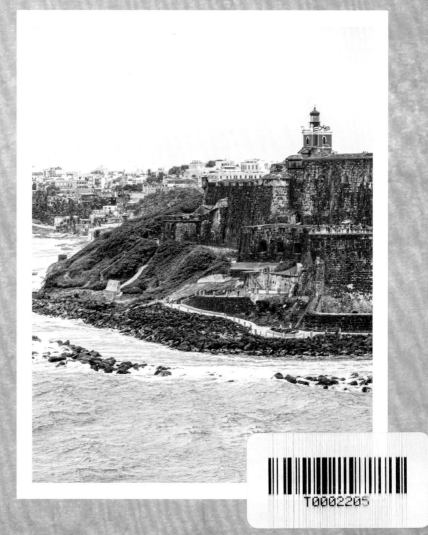

Monika Davies

Consultant

Brian Allman
Principal
Upshur County Schools, West Virginia

Publishing Credits

Rachelle Cracchiolo, M.S.Ed., *Publisher*
Emily R. Smith, M.A.Ed., *SVP of Content Development*
Véronique Bos, *VP of Creative*
Dona Herweck Rice, *Senior Content Manager*
Dani Neiley, *Editor*
Fabiola Sepulveda, *Series Graphic Designer*

Image Credits: p12 Alamy Stock Photo/Photo Resource Hawaii; p15 Alamy Stock Photo/
North Wind Picture Archives; p16 (top) Library of Congress [2004707892]; p16 (bottom)
Library of Congress [LC-D4-8895]; p17 (top) Associated Press; p18 Alamy Stock Photo/
Heritage Image Partnership Ltd; p19 Granger; p20 Cindy Miller Hopkins/DanitaDelimont.
com/"Danita Delimont Photography"/Newscom; p21 United States Navy ID
060920-N-0000X-001; p22 Associated Press; p24 (top) Stefani Reynolds - CNP/Newscom;
p24 (bottom) GDA Photo Service/Newscom; p25 Getty Images/adamkaz; p27 (top) Alamy
Stock Photo/Anders Ryman; p27 (middle) Alamy Stock Photo/Richard Ellis; p27 (bottom)
Alamy Stock Photo/Philip Game; p28 Shutterstock/Paul McKinnon; all other images from
iStock and/or Shutterstock

Library of Congress Cataloging-in-Publication Data

Title: The U.S. territories / Monika Davies.
Description: Huntington Beach, CA : Teacher Created Materials, [2022] |
   Includes index. | Audience: Grades 4-6 | Summary: "State or territory?
   What's the difference in America? There are five main U.S. territories.
   Their geographies are unlike any state. Each has a vibrant culture and
   unique history. Millions of U.S. citizens live in these distinct areas.
   Get to know the five territories in this book-and look ahead to what
   their futures may hold -- Provided by publisher.
Identifiers: LCCN 2022021233 (print) | LCCN 2022021234 (ebook) | ISBN
   9781087691008 (paperback) | ISBN 9781087691169 (ebook)
Subjects: LCSH: United States--Territories and possessions--Juvenile
   literature. | United States--Insular possessions--Juvenile literature.
Classification: LCC F965 .D38 2022 (print) | LCC F965 (ebook) | DDC
   909/.091973--dc23/eng/20220502
LC record available at https://lccn.loc.gov/2022021233
LC ebook record available at https://lccn.loc.gov/2022021234

**Shown on the cover is the Castillo San Felipe
del Morro in San Juan, Puerto Rico.**

5482 Argosy Avenue
Huntington Beach, CA 92649
www.tcmpub.com

ISBN 978-1-0876-9100-8
© 2023 Teacher Created Materials, Inc.

Table of Contents

State or Territory? 4

Unique Cultures and Geography 6

Becoming U.S. Territories 14

Indigenous Peoples. 18

Present-Day Economics. 20

Civic Engagement and Representation 22

Part of America 26

Map It! 28

Glossary. 30

Index. 31

Learn More! 32

a port at St. John's, Antigua

State or Territory?

If asked, many people could draw a map of the United States. A **distinct** shape springs to mind. The sketch would likely include the country's 50 states. Some might think this map is complete. But is there more to America than its states?

The U.S. **Congress** makes decisions for several territories. In total, there are 14 U.S. territories. Some are islands dotted across the Pacific Ocean. Others are islands near the Atlantic. Five of these territories are home to people. No people live in the other U.S. territories.

Asia

• Midway Islands

• Wake Island

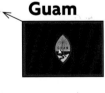

**Northern
Mariana
Islands**

• Johnston Atoll

Guam

Kingman Reef

Palmyra Atoll

Howland Island

Baker Island

Australia

Each one has its own government. Like U.S. states, some territories elect **governors**. With the exception of American Samoa, people who live in a territory are U.S. citizens. They follow American laws. They also pay federal taxes. People who live in American Samoa are considered U.S. **nationals**. Every U.S. citizen is a U.S. national. But not every U.S. national is a U.S. citizen.

Territories are not treated the same as U.S. states. Citizens do not have the same voting rights. They cannot vote for the next president. Territories also lack voting power in Congress. Many people believe this needs to change. But people have different views on how to bring about change for the territories.

North America

Atlantic Ocean

Puerto Rico

U.S. Virgin Islands

Navassa Island

Pacific Ocean

Jarvis Island

American Samoa

South America

Unique Cultures and Geography

The United States is home to a variety of landscapes. Vast mountain ranges seem to touch the sky. Wide plains cover the middle of the country. Waterways such as rivers, lakes, and bayous cross the landscape.

The territories are made of unique **terrain**. For starters, each one is surrounded by ocean. Some are collections of islands. Nearly all have a **tropical** climate. Year-round, the cities in U.S. territories experience warm to hot temperatures.

Like in any place, the people who live in the territories define their home regions. Each territory has its own culture and **customs**. Let's explore each one.

Puerto Rico

Many people think of Puerto Rico as an island. This U.S. territory is located in the Caribbean Sea. Deep waters encircle Puerto Rico. But this territory is an archipelago. An archipelago is a group of islands.

About 190 million years ago, a volcano erupted. This eruption created the group of islands now known as Puerto Rico. Three of the islands are home to people.

The main island is called Puerto Rico. It is home to the bulk of the inhabitants. San Juan, the capital, is also there. Two smaller islands lie to the east. They are named Vieques and Culebra. People live on these islands, too.

San Juan, Puerto Rico

a street in San Juan

PUERTO RICO

ATLANTIC OCEAN

Isabela
SAN JUAN

Aguadilla
Arecibo
Dorado
Carolina
Isla de
Culebra

Isla
Desecheo
San Seastian
Manati
Bayamón
Fajardo

Mayagüez
Utuado
Caguas
Ceiba
Juncos

Río Grande de Añasco

Isla Mona
Adjuntas
Coamo
Aibonito
Humacao
Vieques

San
Germán
Yauco
Cayey
Yabucoa
Isla de
Vieques

Ponce
Guayama

Cabo
Rojo
Santa Isabel
Isla Caja
de Muertos

CARIBBEAN SEA

Tropic Temperatures

The tropics are hot regions! They have some of Earth's warmest temperatures year-round. The average temperatures range between 77 to 82 °F (25 to 28 °C). The tropics get more sun, so their seasons are different from the seasons the rest of the world experiences. The tropics experience wet and dry seasons.

El Yunque National Forest, Puerto Rico

Rugged terrain covers Puerto Rico. Mountains add slopes to the land. Sandy beaches outline the edges of the islands. A tropical rain forest is also here. El Yunque National Forest is full of life. It hosts over 180 animal species!

The people of Puerto Rico are **diverse**. Their heritage is a blend of Taíno, African, and Spanish. The territory has two official languages. Visitors hear both Spanish and English spoken.

Puerto Rico has a vibrant culture. The music and art scenes are bold and colorful. Here, street murals grab the eye. Lively salsa music is often heard. The music offers a fun reason to dance away. There are major festivals with parades and live bands.

Patria

People of Puerto Rico are known for their *patria*. Translated, this means they have a deep love for their home. They are proud of their heritage. They also feel a loyalty to their culture. Some Puerto Ricans move between their home and the mainland United States.

U.S. Virgin Islands

Another U.S. territory lies to the east of Puerto Rico. The Virgin Islands are a chain of islands. There are around 90 in total. Some are part of the U.S. Virgin Islands. Others form the British Virgin Islands. The islands line the top of the Puerto Rico Trench. This is the deepest section of the Atlantic Ocean.

The U.S. Virgin Islands (USVI) is made of three large islands. About 50 smaller islands make up the rest. The largest island is named St. Croix. St. Thomas is the second largest. It is home to the territory's capital city, Charlotte Amalie.

St. Thomas, U.S. Virgin Islands

St. John is the smallest of the three main islands in the USVI. Two-thirds of St. John is protected park land. More than 40 percent of this lies underwater! High hills extend across the other islands.

St. John Carnival

Most of the population is Black or multiethnic. USVI's official music is called *quelbe*. Enslaved people grew and developed *quelbe* music. The music was their way to share stories and jokes with rhythm. *Quelbe* musicians are resourceful and use various items to play music. A sardine tin may serve as their banjo!

The people of USVI also love to have fun. The three main islands each host an annual Carnival. The celebrations last from three to four weeks.

street musicians in St. Thomas

Guam

Guam is in the Pacific Ocean. It is the largest tropical island of the Mariana Islands. This small island is home to Port Apra. This port is an important U.S. **naval** base.

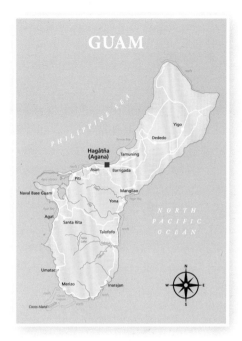

The island's terrain varies widely. To the north, tall cliffs rise high above the ocean. In the south, the landscape is made of savannas. Many tropical plants grow here. Coral reefs also circle this island. Nearly a thousand species of fish live in this vibrant environment.

The biggest ethnic group on Guam is the CHamoru. They are the **Indigenous** people of Guam. About a quarter of the population is Filipino. Hagåtña (huh-GOT-nyuh) is Guam's capital, but not many people live there.

Homegrown Foods

People in Guam also celebrate with festivals. At their parties, there is often a huge table of local treats. The island's most popular dishes are served. These include red rice, chicken with lemon, and grilled seafood. People in Guam also love *fina'denne'* sauce, a fiery addition to any meal.

Northern Mariana Islands

The Northern Mariana Islands are north of Guam. They are also a group of islands. The islands are part of the Mariana Trench. This is an underwater mountain range. Every island is a peak on this range.

Around half the islanders are Asian. About 20 percent are CHamoru. Many residents were born and raised there. Nearly all live on Saipan, one of the islands.

The islanders also love to host festivals. The longest-running one is the Flame Tree Arts Festival. Local art is showcased, and people play both traditional and modern music.

NORTHERN MARIANA ISLANDS

Farallon de Pajaros

Maug Islands

Asuncion

Agrihan

NORTH PACIFIC OCEAN

Pagan

PHILIPPINE SEA

Alamagan

Guguan

Sarigan

Anatahan

Farallon de Medinilla

Saipan ■ Saipan

Aguijan

Tinian

Rota

Hula dancers perform on the island of Saipan.

Spot a Whale

Clear, blue waters surround the Northern Mariana Islands. These waters are where different whale species swim. Visitors can keep an eye out for blue whales, fin whales, humpback whales, sei whales, and sperm whales. All five of these species are **endangered**.

American Samoa

American Samoa is a collection of islands found in the South Pacific Ocean. This territory is made of five volcanic islands. Two **coral atolls** round out the rest of the region. The five islands are where people live.

Coral reefs line the edges of the islands. Plenty of rain falls here. Pago Pago, the capital city, sees 130 inches (330 centimeters) of rain a year!

The islands are home to Samoans. They are a Polynesian people. Their culture is communal, meaning that most Samoans are part of an extended family. These large families live in villages.

Amanave, American Samoa

Becoming U.S. Territories

Every U.S. territory has a rich history. Their customs come from centuries of stories. In some ways, the territories have had similar experiences. Each became a U.S. territory within the last 150 years. Yet none of them has become a U.S. state. Let's look at their connections to the United States.

1898

Puerto Rico and Guam share a piece of history. They both became U.S. territories in the same year. Both were first home to Indigenous peoples. European settlers later arrived. This was in the early 1500s. From then on, both were under Spanish rule.

The year 1898 was a turning point. This year marked the end of the Spanish-American War, which America won. The United States went on to take Puerto Rico and Guam from Spain.

At the time, America saw Puerto Rico as a place to store warships. It was a **strategic** site. Later, in 1917, the Jones-Shafroth Act was passed. The Act granted citizenship to Puerto Rican residents. But Puerto Ricans still lacked many voting powers.

In 1898, Guam also became a U.S. naval station. It was not until 1950 that Guam became an official U.S. territory.

Columbus's Claims

Christopher Columbus was a European explorer. He was once known for "discovering" the New World. He is now remembered for his terrible treatment of the Indigenous peoples he met on his travels. In 1493, he was the first European explorer to discover Puerto Rico and the Virgin Islands. This had an impact on the history of the two regions.

U.S. troops enter Ponce, Puerto Rico, during the Spanish-American War in 1898.

1900

American Samoa is in the Pacific. Many countries wanted control of the area. In the late 1800s, the area became a battleground because three countries wanted control. A war seemed ready to begin, but a typhoon hit the islands. Many lives were lost.

Indigenous chief of American Samoa

The United Kingdom withdrew. The other two countries came to terms. Germany took over the western islands. America took over the eastern one. In 1900, American Samoa became a U.S. territory. The local chiefs **ceded** the island.

1917

Different countries sought to control the Virgin Islands. Spain first claimed the islands. In time, English and French settlers arrived. Later, the islands came under Danish control. In 1917, the United States bought the territory. The plan was to store naval warships there. This was during World War I.

Virgin Islands, about 1917

1976

Northern Marianas was the last to become a U.S. territory. For years, the islands were under Spanish rule. Then came the beginning of the 20th century. The islands were sold to Germany.

The islands faced turmoil during the world wars. During World War I, Japan took control of the islands. World War II saw the islands come under U.S. control. Years later, the islands became a U.S. territory.

U.S. troops invade Saipan.

Organized Territories?

Four of the U.S. territories are organized territories. This means that each one can create a government. Each can also elect a governor to lead them. American Samoa is the only one considered an "unincorporated, unorganized" territory. This territory's residents are American nationals.

Indigenous Peoples

Each territory was first home to Indigenous peoples. This includes the Taíno. The Taíno is a group of Arawak Indians. They were the first to live on the lands of Puerto Rico. For centuries, they grew sweet potatoes and beans. The Arawak tribes came up with the words *canoe* and *hammock*. Their canoes could seat more than 100 people!

The Taíno were known for their creativity. They developed games using rubber balls. Their pottery pieces and cotton belts had complex designs.

The U.S. Virgin Islands were also first home to Arawak peoples. They were peaceful and may have come from Venezuela to the islands. Arawak pottery has been **excavated** from different parts of the islands. But little is known about the lives of the Arawak in the past. Carib people came later to the islands. Their arrival marked the end of the Arawak peoples on the islands.

Arawak Indians, 1854

native peoples of Pago Pago,
American Samoa, 1940

In Guam, the CHamoru were the first to settle on the land. They first came more than 3,500 years ago. They came from other islands in Southeast Asia. They built unique *latte* houses in their villages. These structures are only seen in Guam. *Latte* houses are built on distinctive stone pillars. Structures made of wood and thatch roofs were balanced on top of the pillars. *Latte* houses are still seen as a symbol of strength for CHamoru peoples.

To this day, many of Guam's people are CHamoru. Northern Marianas is also home to CHamoru peoples.

Samoans

Polynesians first settled on the islands of American Samoa. This was around 1000 BCE. The territory's residents are mainly descendants of Polynesian people. Many are **fluent** in the Samoan language.

Present-Day Economics

The U.S. Territories have some parallels with one another. This is true of their economies, too. For one, all rely on tourism. For instance, the Virgin Islands are known for sandy beaches. People enjoy the warm weather. Some come for sport fishing. Millions visit every year.

Puerto Rico also hosts many visitors. People from the U.S. mainland travel there often. Cruise ships are a common sight among the islands. The Northern Marianas also welcome a lot of guests. Their casinos are a big draw.

Paradise Point, St. Thomas skyride

U.S. Naval Base Guam

Goods and Services

Exports are goods and services made in one location. These are then sold to other locations. Exports help drive an economy. Puerto Rico has many exports. Chemicals and computers are two of them. The Virgin Islands exports rum.

Guam has a key U.S. naval station. Thousands of members of the military live there. A lot of money comes to the island from national defense. Tourism is also important to the island.

American Samoa has a traditional economy. About 90 percent of the land is communal. Large groups own and share the land. Many workers are fishers. Others prepare the fish for eating. Canned tuna is their main export.

Hurricane Maria

Hurricane Maria roared through Puerto Rico and the U.S. Virgin Islands in 2017. The natural disaster destroyed housing. It also led to huge power outages and **contaminated** drinking water. The hurricane's impact cost Puerto Rico $90 billion. These issues led many Puerto Ricans to move to the U.S. mainland.

Civic Engagement and Representation

People of the territories are U.S. citizens. Like many citizens, they are committed to their communities. They work to make a difference. They want their communities to have bright and healthy futures.

Every year, there is an International Coastal Cleanup™. People across the planet head to their countries' coastlines. Their goal is to remove trash from waterways. Puerto Rico hosts a massive cleanup every year. Thousands volunteer to help out. Beaches, rivers, and parks are cleaned.

The Community Foundation of the Virgin Islands (CFVI) is made of local leaders. The CFVI offers services to islanders. They also provide grants. Grants are amounts of money given to a group for a purpose. Some grants are given as scholarships. These fund education for students. The CFVI hopes to help islanders live their "highest quality of life."

International Coastal Cleanup Day in Fajardo, Puerto Rico

Island Girl Power is a group in Guam. Their mission is to "empower, encourage, and inspire" young girls. The group hosts activities, such as dance lessons. They want to provide positive role models for young girls. Carlotta Leon Guerrero is the group's founder. She believes "women are the backbone of a community." She wants to help make "girls strong at an early age."

the effects of Hurricane Maria

Climate Concerns

Climate change is a concern for everyone. But certain areas are more vulnerable to its harmful effects. This includes the tropical U.S. territories. Each island is small and remote. Pollution has already put stress on their unique ecosystems. Climate change could have a devastating impact on the territories in the future.

Representation Matters

The U.S. territories have rich histories. Their communities are vibrant. Each one is a part of America. Yet there are key differences between territories and U.S. states. Many of these differences are civic matters.

Stacey Plaskett, United States Delegate of the Virgin Islands

In America, citizens have the right to vote. This is an important right. It is a key part of the country's democracy. Voting is how citizens have an impact on government decisions. They vote for people to represent them in government. Voters elect people who will stand up for what matters to them.

The territories are home to U.S. citizens and nationals. But they lack the same voting rights as people who live in U.S. states. There are over 3.5 million citizens in the territories. They are not allowed to vote in national elections. This means they cannot vote for the next president.

None of the territories have a senator. Senators are members of the U.S. Congress. They make the laws in America. These laws apply to the territories, too. With no senators, the territories have little say in the laws that affect them.

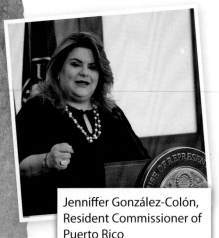

Jenniffer González-Colón, Resident Commissioner of Puerto Rico

Each territory can elect a **representative** to the U.S. House. But these representatives have limited powers. They cannot vote on **bills**.

What about Samoans?

People who live in American Samoa are U.S. nationals, not U.S. citizens. They are asked for loyalty to America. But they are not given the same citizenship rights as other Americans. If someone from Samoa wants to move to the U.S. mainland, they must go through an immigration process—even though they were born in a U.S. territory.

Part of America

Hurricane Maria hit Puerto Rico in 2017. Nearly 3,000 Americans died. It was an immense tragedy. For some U.S. citizens though, it was the first time they'd heard that Puerto Ricans are U.S. citizens. A *New York Times* poll asked U.S. mainland citizens about Puerto Rico. Around half did not know that people born in Puerto Rico are U.S. citizens.

When some people think of America, they picture the 50 states. The territories are located away from the U.S. mainland. But the U.S. Virgin Islands and Puerto Rico are very close to the mainland, much more so than Hawai'i. They are part of the picture, too. And each place struggles to have its voice heard.

Millions of people call the territories home. They come from different walks of life. Some love to celebrate with big festivals or parties. They are proud of their histories. And they are all Americans.

Many agree it's time for a change. It's time for the people of the territories to have the full rights of U.S. citizenship. But what does the future look like for the territories? There is no one way forward. Hopefully, each one will have the freedom of choice in the near future.

The Stories of the Territories

When people live far from us, we can sometimes lose sight of the richness of their human experiences. People in the territories have struggles. They, too, have loved ones. Many of them want to vote and know that their votes count. This is true for all U.S. citizens. How can you learn more about the people of the different territories?

Map It!

We have spent a lot of time learning about the territories. It is now time to map them out. Better yet, it is time to collaborate! Grab a friend or two for some political map-making.

1. Find a large piece of paper and a couple of pens.
2. First, roughly sketch the area of the United States. Label the nearby oceans.
3. There are five main U.S. territories. Make a list of their names. Some of them are made of many islands. Write the names of all the major islands where people live in each territory.
4. Next, look up the population numbers for each territory. How many people live in each region? Write the total number next to each territory's name.
5. Look up the territories on a map. Where are they in relation to the United States mainland? Sketch their locations, and make sure to include all major islands.
6. Label each territory and every major island. Include the population numbers for each territory.
7. Bonus question: What state is about the same size as Puerto Rico?

St. Thomas, U.S. Virgin Islands

American Samoa

Guam

Northern Mariana Islands

Puerto Rico

U.S. Virgin Islands

Glossary

bills—written descriptions of new laws being proposed that lawmakers must vote on

ceded—gave control of something to another group

Congress—the U.S. Senate and House of Representatives

contaminated—made dangerous by adding something harmful to it

coral atolls—ring-shaped coral reefs or islands

customs—behaviors that are usual and traditional among people in a particular group or area

distinct—not like others

diverse—made up of people or things that are different from each other

endangered—relating to an endangered species; in danger of going extinct

excavated—uncovered by digging away and taking out the soil that covers it

fluent—able to speak a language very well with ease

governors—people who are the leaders of state or territory governments

Indigenous—from or native to a particular area

nationals—citizens

naval—related to a country's navy or military ships

representative—a person or group that advocates and acts for another person or group

strategic—useful or vital in achieving a plan or an outcome

terrain—areas of land that share certain features

tropical—relating to the tropics, the part of the world near the equator where the weather is very warm

San Juan, Puerto Rico

Index

American Samoa, 4–5, 13, 16–17, 19, 21, 25

Arawak, 18

Atlantic Ocean, 9

Caribbean Sea, 6

CHamoru, 11–12, 19

Charlotte Amalie, 9

climate change, 23

Columbus, Christopher, 14

Congress, 4–5, 24

El Yunque National Forest, 8

Flame Tree Arts Festival, 12

Germany, 16–17

Guam, 4–5, 11–12, 14, 19, 21, 23

Hagåtña, 11

Hurricane Maria, 21, 23, 26

Northern Mariana Islands, 4–5, 12–13, 17, 19–20

Pacific Ocean, 4, 11, 13, 16

Port Apra, 11

Puerto Rico, 4–9, 14–15, 18, 20–22, 24, 26

representation, 22–25

San Juan, 6–7

Taíno, 8, 18

United Kingdom, 16

U.S. Virgin Islands, 4–5, 9–10, 18, 21, 26

Learn More!

The United States has a House of Representatives. This is an elected group of people. They help create and pass federal laws. Four of the main territories each has a delegate in the House of Representatives. Puerto Rico has a resident commissioner. Each one represents their territory—but they lack voting rights in the House. They can sit in on discussions. But their list of tasks is very different from that of other House members.

✳ Research the current delegates for the territories.

✳ Create poster profiles for each one.

- What are their names?

- Where is their hometown?

- What do they think about statehood for their home territory?

✳ See if you can find quotations or pictures for each poster.

Puerto Rico Capitol in San Juan